Melancholy and the Occasional Smile

SHANNA WIELGOSZ

BookLeaf Publishing

India | USA | UK

Presentation by *BookLeaf Publishing*

Web: www.bookleafpub.com

E-mail: info@bookleafpub.com

ISBN: 9789363308244

First edition 2024

DEDICATION

Dedicated to my four precious gifts, Acacia, Lyric, Lyla, and Harlow,

You have transformed my life in ways I never thought possible, filling my world with laughter, joy, and magic. Your unique spirits, curiosity, and love inspire me every day to chase my dreams and never give up.

To my dear children, I offer these words: always follow your hearts, chase your passions, and never let fear hold you back. The world needs your light, your creativity, and your love.

I love you all dearly, more than words can express.

May this book be a reminder that your dreams are worth chasing, and that your love and support mean the world to me.

ACKNOWLEDGEMENT

Thanks to Lyric Greathouse and Harry Stone for bringing my cover art vision to life with their incredible design talents. I appreciate your hard work and creativity!

Corridor

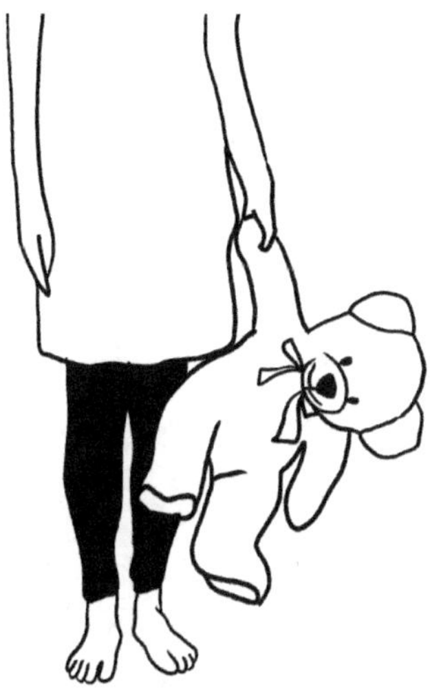

I drag my hand down the sides of the corridor
It's pitch black and all I can hear is the sound of
my heel colliding with the floor
I hum to myself
Listening for my name….
Anticipating someone might need me.

Several years of lullabies later
I've yet to hear it called.

I've grown familiar with each crevice of the wall
I trace my fingers along them
trying to decipher what caused the damage.

Some are deeper… some longer
I place my forehead against the surface and hum
louder.

I've all but accepted my fate.
The melody makes it easier to swallow.

Mother

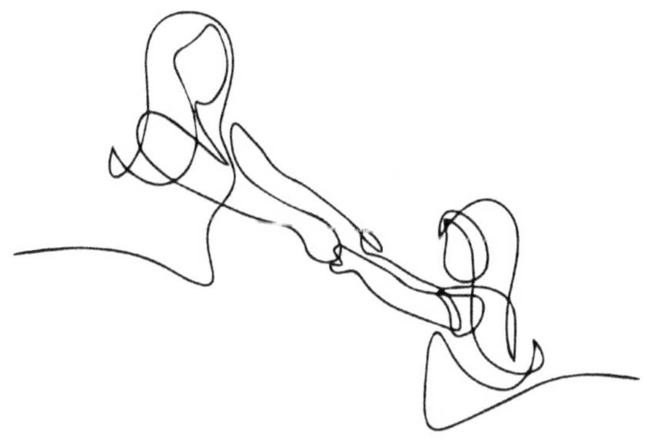

I watch you wither
as time slowly takes your mind
I hear past laughter
that the pain hasn't redefined
I will miss your smile; it reminds me of mine.

Underneath the haze
I see you as a girl
Lost
Trying to find her place in this world.
I've taken your broken pieces
And wove them with mine
Following rotted footsteps
Listlessly falling in line.

Despite it all, I love you
Despite it all, I care

Time is limited
So I force myself to heal.
Shadows lurk around me
Grey is all I feel

I may only ever be half of me
But half of me you'll have

Footsteps

Numb, I turn away
Tears stained by the color of my heart
Seep down my cheeks

I close my eyes and imagine
Every step you would take
Every decision, every turn
Even the ones that left me to burn

The fire never hurt me;
It only helped make me strong
Engulfed in flames is where I grew my heart.
But what was it about me
That you found so wrong?

These are the questions I don't get to ask
Too risky when you're trying to erase the past

Stay

Just stand there and look pretty
Forget your hands are wet with guilt
Stand there looking innocent
Forget you've been a player in this filth

You've never been one to see
Deny, Deny, Deny
But I see you clearly
You're the only one on your side

You never were content with gentle words of
dull
No, you exposed her insides
Feasted while she was weak
Gun to head
As she helplessly complied

Now she's gone and you're to blame
Stained
With the nothingness of the girl you liked to
love this way

North Star

I've got a long way to go
to cleanse this soul of mine
I'm almost certain the dark
and my smile are intertwined

Always deceiving my progress

I put one foot in front of the other
slowly walk away from the
beautiful life I've built
with one beautiful lie after another

Your tears shower the ground
but I can no longer be bothered
You fumble with why
I'll never tell you how much
I wanted to stay
I would have followed you everywhere
I would have followed you anywhere

Flawed

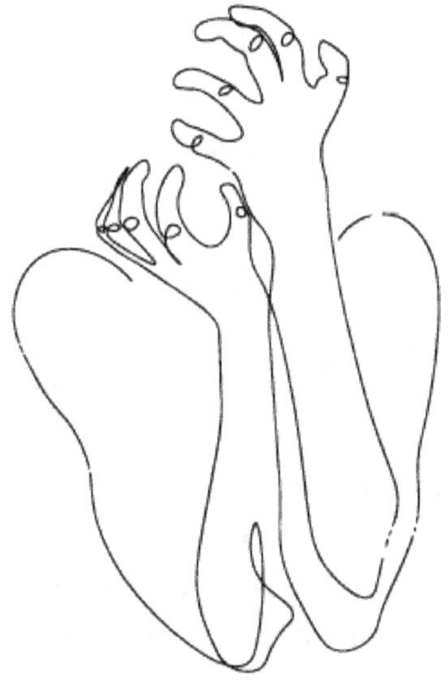

I see them
I feel them
I'm reminded of them every time an opportunity
passes me by—
The opportunity to belong
To be at peace knowing there are hands
to catch me the same way I make mine available
for others to fall.

Maybe my downfall was catching too often

I found beauty in my own downfalls so I could
bring meaning to my mind.
My compassion and understanding of others
grew as my hands withered.
Unable to hold as much as they once did, I feel
the decomposition move to the meticulously
placed ribbon that I've used to keep myself
together.

Slowly it unravels, leaving my most concealed
parts exposed.
I often wonder if it was all for nothing.
A lesson I was meant to learn from a past life.
It's been lost on me.

My biggest accomplishment is learning all too
slowly I am not meant to be here any longer. A
lesson I should have learned long ago.

Pebbles

Once upon a time, I was led to believe being a
rock was spoken about with positivity.
I see now being a rock means you've hardened
to the world just to be kicked or tossed into the
depths of someone else's river.
I no longer wish to be a rock.
I only wish to be free.

Anchor

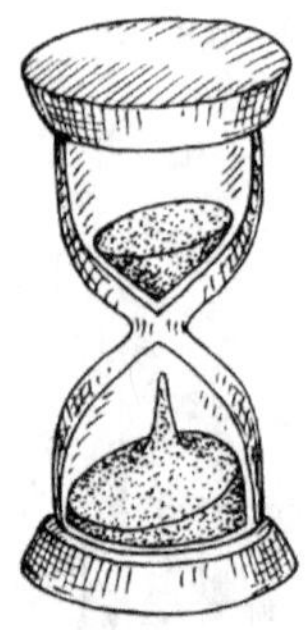

The disappointment seeps into your sighs
I've been here before, exhausting someone until
Loving me is a distant memory
It's not like they didn't try
I'm impossible
Effort is always wasted on me
Regret lingers around me like a shadow
If it's not today, it will be tomorrow
You'll wish you never stumbled

I put my phone down
Willing my fingers to drop
We don't have to say anymore
I can't chase your thoughts
I can't chase you
I would try
God knows I would try for you

But what good would it do to be the one
to catch someone running from themselves
I ache because I know what quiet moments do
I know what comes next, as much as you don't
want it to.
Suddenly, the anchor isn't made of metal and I
see the string
I sit staring at it curiously
Will I even see it unravel?
Or will it wait for me to forget about it and come
undone in the middle of the night…

Veils

My reflection was anything and everything short of human.
I struggled to see what it was that some would fake love for, hate me for, and some just wanted to possess without looking inside.

I assume by now I was either convincingly hollow or they knew the work that would be involved if they were to twist the lid.

Worth touching, worth looking at, but never worth knowing.

I can thank my repulsion for saving me from
being handled by hands that would never care.
Unfortunately for me, my lack of interest added
to the lure
and not every caress needed a yes.

Exceptions

You said you wanted to remain professional
But there they are
Displayed on the forbidden page
You speak down on them, claim they're not
special
Yet every exception is written in their names.

Masks

Morbidities traced wounds
leaving behind sparkling trails of black
Where other people lacked the ability to see the
beauty in the downfall, I built my entire life
around never rising
Allowing myself to drown in the deepest parts of
my mind.
Drinking in and becoming intoxicated with
being 6 feet under while still breathing
I assigned traits I'd never let myself escape

Wearing every broken piece of me like a badge
of honor, a name tag…. and at times my own
handcrafted armor.

In the real world I allowed myself to succeed.
Knowing the girl on the outside wasn't the same
as the girl on the inside
I'd wear masks
Carefully labeling each one—
Successful…. Popular…. Smart…. Talented….
Carefree

Every new skill was gained and used to find a
love
I should have been given freely upon taking my
first breath.
I often wondered why the universe allows entire
family structures to crumble beneath the weight
of losing someone significant…. Someone who
mattered … while keeping me grounded in
places I'd never grow… using air better spent on
the worthy.

Gray

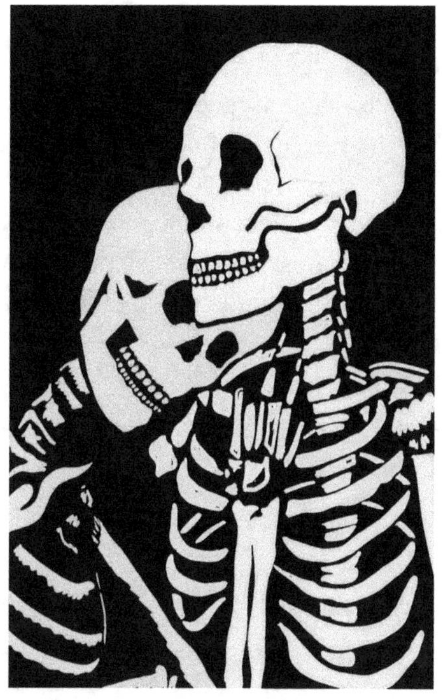

Some of us don't want to be saved
Some of us want to dance with our demons until
we find peace
Hold hands with what scares us until fear no
longer exists

Happy is not the only beauty this world holds
When you travel into the gray you find your
resilience

You find what keeps you whole
It is pain that sparks anger
Anger that sparks movement
and movement that guides us to success
What a sad day for the monster
when we turn back in relief to be away from it
For it was he who held your hand and lit the
flame
that guided you to your smile
One day I wish to see our monsters thanked, a
knowing nod of gratitude gestured their way
when our path clears

Walls

I feel it closing in
Dread.. the need to retreat
I went back too far into the memories, to a time
you were happy.
Lust and curiosity driving you
Not built for long-term
but you can never tell that to a restless heart
I wanted you to love me
I wanted to feel like a dream
For a time both were true
Until you got to know me

Slow fade

I replay old messages as if you're gone
Our voices meet daily but the passion you once
met me with no longer reverberates through the
line
What was once spoken vampishly causing
Syllables to coil around my loins have gone
listless
You're here, sure
But not with the fire that once drove you to me
and me to desperation
Will I become like the others?

Unmet
Body willing with a crushed heart in hand?

25

Pathways

I think you were put into my life to re-light my
path
Not a path towards forever
But a path that opens up my heart
where I can use words to paint a picture of how
crushed I feel
A path guided by pieces of me I gave to you
that were so carelessly thrown back
Being complacent never made me creative
Being creative came from my pain
Shadow work led me to peace
and in that peace, I lost the way to describe the
ache so beautifully.

Sometimes the slow drip of our souls
harmonizes with the pulsing beat of heartbreak
It creates an orchestra for those living in the
shadows
So in the end, did you do me a favor by leading
me into nights filled with tears in the middle of
October, my favorite month?
Or will this lead me to my symphony?
As long as you're on my mind I'll write, sing
and paint.
Picking up the broken pieces of me along the
way.
When I reach the end of this path it will be your
memory I'd discard
You, that I throw away….
preparing myself to be feasted on again by
another one like you
knowing at the end I'll be ok and I'll find even
more beauty in the pain.

Dream

Great things take time
It's in moments like this, as I stare into space
Letting my mind wander, that I can feel your
roots being planted in my heart
Vines made from your voice snake their way
through me
Blooming so rapidly the earth crumbles beneath
my feet.

I breathe deep

A lesson disguised as a person to teach me
patience—

Patience with myself
Patience with the world around me
Patience with fire

I can not touch you today;
I can not touch you tomorrow.
Yet I'm driven by a desire so strong that I can
almost feel your arms wrapped around my waist

I slow my breathing to match a heartbeat I have
yet to hear, though it fills the space around me
I sit in silence listening to the internal roar
Surrendering intrinsically to the pace

Eagerly I await nights, I close my eyes and open
them to meet yours.
I smile as your lips press against mine.
I fall into you
Wishing I could stay
In a few short hours you'll be ripped from
dreams
And placed miles away

Daydreams and midnight drives

I sit here trying to write and I just can't seem to make all the pieces fit.
I want so desperately to describe the feeling of leaving my body in slumber and opening my eyes during a late-night drive.
Hanging my arm out the window as you snake your way around curves. Watching trees fly by, staring up at the stars…
Turning my attention to you when I feel you twist your fingers through mine.
Taking it all in as if it's reality

You're carrying on about something and as
much as I want to hear you, the music playing
takes my mind elsewhere.
All I can manage to focus on is the way your lips
move when you talk
the excitement in your eyes and your voice…..
uhhh your voice.
I may not hear a word you're saying but it
speaks to me in a way that sends waves crashing
through my chest.
Like clockwork, you seem to be able to read my
thoughts, and pull over to the side of the road.
Guiding me into your arms as we slow dance in
the illumination of the headlights.

I lay my head on your chest, breathing in the
way you smell.
Terrified something in real life will wake me
from this moment.
You lean in to kiss me and I try hard to
memorize every detail of how your mouth feels
and tastes on mine, hoping to take as much as
possible back with me so I can daydream about
it tomorrow.
I want to stay here, I want to belong here… .
I don't think there will ever be a day where I can
paint in enough colors or use words to describe
the way my heart loves yours.

I don't even think the pain of all my heartbreaks
combined could match the intensity of my pulse
when I think of you.
Something stirs outside me and I know it's only
a few moments before I'll have to leave you
here, knowing I'll fight like hell to return
tomorrow.

One day

Patiently
Until the ocean falls and our worlds meet
I'll wait
Dancing along the edge of sanity and reason
An imagination full of vivid pictures of what's
to come, keeping me company.

Catalyst

He has a way of making every break feel
intentional
Beauty in every crack
Once his words heal me
Who will I be if I'm not broken...

Gravity

I've never been so willing to hand my heart over
to be caged

You're too far to hold my hand
So I'll use it to write your name in swirling
letters

Every loop placed on paper in reverie

Every daydream the same
You and me
Drives, dancing, laughter and silent nights lost in
our own thoughts.

One day I'll look across the room over the
flickering flame of a candle near gone

Studying the way you look through the glow it's
casted
Worry has faded from your face
Replaced with content from a life finally lived

I allow my mind to tiptoe through years of
memories, to the day that holds that fate-driven
conversation

11:11

I smile internally, warmth filling my chest
You could have never convinced me before that
day that I would have willingly handed my heart
over to be caged

Wings withered from a long flight I called my
life
Finally in hands that held me softly
Soft enough to allow my mind to piece itself
back together
Soothed by a voice that whispered their
sentiment
Every kiss
Every delicate word
Every sync
Built my new home

Hand in hand
A pumpkin and her muffin man.